D0478632

CUT-FLOWER ROSES

CUT-FLOWER ROSES

by rayford clayton reddell

photographs by saxon holt

CHRONICLE BOOKS

SAN FRANCISCO

Text copyright © 1999 by Rayford Clayton Reddell.
Photographs copyright © 1999 by Saxon Holt.
All rights reserved. No part of this book may be reproduced in any form
without written permission from the publisher.

Library of Congress Cataloging-in-Publication Data:
Reddell, Rayford Clayton.
Cut-flower roses / by Rayford Clayton Reddell; photographs by Saxon Holt.
p. cm. Includes index. ISBN 0-8118-2270-2 (hc)
1. Rose culture. 2. Roses—Varieties. 3. Cut flowers I. Title.
SB411.R385 1999 635.9'33734—dc21 97-19182 CIP

Printed in Singapore.

Cover and book design by Gregory Design, San Francisco.

The photographer would like to thank Ann Leyhe for styling and scouting assistance,
Polly Harrington for arrangements, and those gardeners who grew the roses and provided
assistance: Cappie Garrett, Allmond Bayard, Eleanor Moscow, David Alosi, Katie Trefethen,
Phyllis Saccani, Keeyla Meadows, Freeland Tanner, Susan David, Empire Mine State Park,
Garden Valley Ranch, Jim Lang, John Dallas, Lisa Ledson, and Claire Leyhe.

Distributed in Canada by Raincoast Books
8680 Cambie Street
Vancouver, British Columbia V6P 6M9

10 9 8 7 6 5 4 3 2 1

Chronicle Books
85 Second Street
San Francisco, CA 94105

www.chroniclebooks.com

This book is dedicated to Sally Jordan,

a beloved rosebuddy

who shares my deep affection for good cut-flower roses

and has a model garden to prove it.

TABLE OF CONTENTS

INTRODUCTION

From the time I carefully planted my very first rosebush and gave it all the love I knew how, its blossoms were what I was really after. When I sprayed, fed, and generally coddled my rose garden, I did so not because I cared deeply for the somewhat stiff plants, but rather because my thirst for their flowers seemed unquenchable.

Although my love affair with roses began modestly in a 20-foot-by-40-foot garden in San Francisco, before I was finished with that little plot, I'd managed to cram in 140 bushes. Since I lived in fear of never having enough blossoms, I catered to the plants' every need and fed them like royalty. In response, they bloomed their heads off.

I gave roses to everyone I knew. Friends called me weeks before parties to invite me, then casually asked if I might have some extra roses just then. For six months of the year, I did.

One day a friend said to me, "You know, you and your beloved blossoms are problems to deal with. I'm having a dinner party and I want nothing so much as some of your roses, but I hate to keep asking. You won't let me pay you, and I'm beginning to feel guilty."

I decided to test the possibility of selling my garden roses. If it worked, I thought to myself, it would be a dandy way to grow beyond my meager 140 plants, which were clearly no longer enough.

Fortunately, I lived near one of San Francisco's finest florists, who agreed to try selling my roses on consignment. They were a hit from the get-go and I began looking for land in nearby Sonoma County (where Luther Burbank got his start), eventually finding the location of my dreams in Petaluma, an idyllic Victorian town just 37 miles north of the Golden Gate Bridge.

Although I started Garden Valley Ranch with a modest planting of 1,200 bushes, in no time at all it was clear that this was a hobby destined to go bananas and I constantly found new sites for more roses. And soon, besides continuing to sell them locally, we began shipping blossoms around the country to the wholesale floral trade. Now I'm more or less content with something in excess of 8,000 bushes and I can truthfully say that the ranch has surpassed my wildest aspirations.

To this day, however, my continuing motivation for growing roses is their blossoms— more specifically fragrant, large, long-stemmed, and, most of all, long-lasting ones. In addition to operating a test garden for the All-America Rose Selection process, I evaluate other roses headed down the pike, continually in search of new varieties that meet my piggy demands. If they don't, I stick with those already proven true.

Growing garden roses commercially for their cut flowers, I've learned that it's not enough to identify the right varieties to cultivate. One must also learn how to coerce blossoms into extended vase life. It's time to share those tricks of the trade.

harvesting

I want to hang my head in shame when I think about how I once harvested my roses. It was bad enough that I cut blooms any time of day I felt like, worse yet I plunked them into a bucket of water I dragged around with me through the garden. As often as not, I ended up spilling the bucket of water and whatever number of rose blossoms it held at that moment. All in all, rose harvests in those days were messy.

Some years later, a respected rosarian in San Francisco told me about the benefits of recutting rose stems under water.

"When roses are cut dry from the bush, air bubbles form in their stems," she explained. "If allowed to remain, those air bubbles travel up the stem, and when they hit the bloom, it keels over."

She went on to assure me that cutting stems under water wasn't nearly as messy as it sounded and advised me to use wicker baskets to gather rose blossoms in and to layer the blooms so that they didn't crush each other. Then to take them into the house.

I was instructed to put some tap water in a bowl and, one at a time, immerse stems into the bowl. Next, using sharp shears, I was to recut ¼ inch off each stem while it was still under water.

"Recutting stems under water seals them and air bubbles can't form. Trust me," she exhorted, "you'll double the life of your blooms."

She was entirely correct, of course, and I follow that advice to this day. But before I tell you how else to extend bloom life (see page 12), it's important that you understand when and how to best harvest roses.

At Garden Valley Ranch, we harvest roses in either early morning or late afternoon, when stems hold maximum water. We cut roses as tight in bud as possible, but that is entirely dependent on variety; some varieties can be cut when buds are tight, others require maturity.

The landmarks for making judicious decisions for when to cut a rose are the sepals—those leaflike coverings of rosebuds. Sepals develop just under rosebuds and join their tips over swelling blooms. When buds develop to the stage that the leaflets can no longer contain them, the sepals begin to unfurl. In some varieties, the sepals put on quite an architectural show, often rivaling their blossoms.

Once sepals have unfurled and buds start to open, blooms can be cut. Precisely how far buds need to open before cutting is recommended differs among varieties. If cut too soon, blossoms of some varieties won't continue to mature in the vase; if cut too late, others will have a greatly shortened vase life.

As for stem length, that too is varietal. Some roses produce blossoms on amazingly long stems (often nearing 3 feet); others are disappointingly short stemmed. Unless a plant seems stressed, I recommend cutting stems as long as you like. The only cardinal rule to be followed is to make all cuts above a set of five or more leaves and above a leaflet set facing *outward* from the center of the bush—the direction in which you want replacement roses to grow.

Following the advice of my original guru, I recommend recutting all stems under water as soon as possible after taking them from their mother bushes. But I strongly urge that you go a step further. Rather than plunging them into just any water, make certain to use hot water (stems absorb hot water more quickly than cold) and bleach (household bleach works perfectly well at a rate of ½ ounce per 8 gallons or two to three drops per quart).

The reason bleach is so important to vase life is because roses, like other woody-stemmed flowers such as camellias and azaleas, take so long to mature that their stems become coated with bacteria. Unless a biocide such as bleach is added to water used for conditioning roses, stems won't be able to take a proper drink because bacteria will be clogging their tips.

Allow the water to return to room temperature before removing freshly cut roses from their containers. Then recut the stems once again and put them into water fortified with floral preservatives.

Commercial preservatives work, but if none is on hand, a homemade brew of 1 teaspoon sugar per quart of water works perfectly well. Add a few drops of household bleach to this mixture as well, just to make certain that all unwanted bacteria are killed and stems won't get clogged.

Ideally, preservatives and bleach should be mixed in $105°F$ water (typical hot kitchen tap temperature) and rose blossoms should be immersed halfway up their stems. If the containers are left to cool overnight in the darkest spot available, by the next morning stems will be turgid and can be moved around out of water with no worries of wilting.

You can gild the lily even further, of course. If you seek the longest bloom life possible, repeat the procedure of recutting stems under water every other day, changing water, preservatives, and bleach as well. Going to such bother will result in rose blossoms that last well in a vase for up to two weeks (some varieties even longer).

Before recommending specific roses with true lasting qualities, I must confess that several of my very favorite cut-flower roses are omitted from this text. In an earlier book in this series, I discussed All-America Roses that get my vote for immortality. Some of them do so because of their amazing life as cut flowers.

Except for 'Fame!', an All-America Selection for 1998, I've gone out of my way to avoid suggesting certain varieties for cut flowers because I've already praised them as All-Americas. To make certain you're not missing out on great cut-flower roses, however, please take a look at *All-America Roses*, the first book in this *A Passion for Roses* series.

Otherwise, the following list is my personal selection of 40 roses I believe outdo themselves as cut flowers:

Abraham Darby	Maggie Barry
Alchemist	Magic Carrousel
America	Minnie Pearl
Berries and Cream	New Day
Chicago Peace	Playboy
Crystalline	Precious Platinum
Dainty Bess	Prima Donna
Elina	Pristine
Evening Star	Purple Tiger
Fair Bianca	Royal Sunset
Fame!	Sally Holmes
Gene Boerner	Sea Pearl
Gold Medal	Sexy Rexy
Gruss an Aachen	Sparrieshoop
Iceberg	Summer Fashion
Ingrid Bergman	Summer's Kiss
Jean Kenneally	Sunset Celebration
Just Joey	Swan
L.D. Braithwaite	Variegata di Bologna
LeAnn Rimes	White Delight

David Austin's English roses have been insanely popular ever since they were introduced in the early 1960s, entirely due to Austin's amazing success in combining the best of two rose worlds. Like heirloom roses, Austin's creations are wondrously formed and deliciously fragrant. Like modern hybrids, they flower nonstop.

While the vast majority of Austin's creations have an heirloom rose (as old as Gallicas) as one parent and a modern rose as another, to create 'Abraham Darby', Austin crossed two modern roses whose blossoms had classic "old rose" qualities—the Floribunda 'Yellow Cushion' and the modern climber 'Aloha'.

'Abraham Darby' is a sturdy lad, with shrubs that grow up to 5 feet. Although plants are shapely and foliage glossy, the blooms are the ticket—large, deeply cupped, loosely petaled, and fragrant as a honey pot. Perhaps most appealing of all is color. The insides of the petals are peachy pink; the outsides are yellow. As blossoms mature, the center petals reflex and segment themselves into dazzling color combinations.

Give Mr. Darby some extra time to mature on his bushes. Give the sepals time, too. Not only should they be fully reflexed, the outer row of petals should begin to clearly separate. Then cut blossoms freely, confident of a splendid show yet to come.

ALCHEMIST

Hybridized in 1956 by the formidable German family of Kordes, 'Alchemist' is registered as a Shrub rose, which indeed it is; and a hefty one at that, hefty enough to happily substitute for a short climber.

Cut-flower rose aficionados find but one fault with 'Alchemist', but it's a rather serious one—flowering is only once a year. Still, it's a majestic and extended season of bloom and the heart-stopping blossoms somehow compensate for their relative infrequency.

Blossoms of 'Alchemist' take so long to fully mature that you'll get to know them intimately before their show has concluded. Because they last such an eternity, they must build and store sufficient energy to see maturity through, which means they must be left on their mother plants longer than most other roses.

When deciding whether or not to harvest, keep in mind that, properly matured, blossoms resemble exaggerated Victorian satin pincushions. For such voluminous domes to develop, blooms should never be harvested until they have reached at least one-third of their potential mass.

Although blossoms are sharply fragrant from the start, they undergo dramatic color changes on their way to maturity. Petals begin life yolk yellow, but by the time they are big enough to scroll to the size of large saucers, they turn handsome shades of apricot and gold.

A M E R I C A

In tribute to his country's bicentennial celebration, Bill Warriner of Jackson & Perkins presented rosedom with a lovely gift—'America', a climbing rose for all time. In response, the prestigious All-America Rose Selections, Incorporated granted the new rose an All-America award in 1976. Only one other climber had ever before copped the coveted endorsement: 'Golden Showers', in 1957.

Warriner chose 'Fragrant Cloud' to mother his creation—a wise choice indeed, considering that many people believe 'Fragrant Cloud' to be the most deeply perfumed rose ever. Thankfully, the heady fragrance was passed on from mother to child.

Color is similar, too. While the American Rose Society has registered 'Fragrant Cloud' as orange-red, 'America' is deemed orange-pink. In truth, both roses are somewhat salmon, although 'America' is the more purely colored.

When they read that blossoms of 'America' have 43 petals each, rosarians who garden in colder-than-average climates shy from it, in favor of more lightly petaled varieties. That's a mistake. I know for a fact, because I first grew 'America' in San Francisco, which is where I lived at the time of its introduction. As you know, San Francisco summers are chilly indeed, but 'America' took to them well and blossoms matured fully and beautifully.

When Pernille Olesen of Denmark looked among her seedlings some years ago, she spotted a variety whose variegated blossoms pleased her enough that she grew it on as a test plant. That pleased her, too, and she sent plants to America, where she intended to introduce her find as a Floribunda. To everyone's eventual delight, the new rose didn't thrive as a shrub. Instead, it climbed vigorously to span more than 15 feet. In 1997 the serendipitous find was introduced by Weeks Roses as a Climbing rose named 'Berries and Cream'.

Almost everyone who sees my plants of 'Berries and Cream' says the same thing—"That rose looks just like 'Rosa Mundi'," referring to the classic pink-and-white Gallica rose. They're correct, it truly does.

Like those of 'Rosa Mundi', blossoms of 'Berries and Cream' are madly splashed shades of pink and soft white, no two alike. Although 'Berries and Cream' isn't nearly as fragrant as its ancestor, it handily makes up for its relative scentlessness by flowering all summer long.

Even though I'm certain I could disbud for one-to-a-stem blossoms, I don't. The clusters of blossoms are so lovely that I prefer removing terminal (centermost) buds, looking forward to harvesting sprays on long cutting stems.

Certain roses are famous for their affinity for producing sports—spontaneous mutations of growth whose blossoms are distinctly dissimilar from those of the parent bush, perhaps as different as black-red from icy-white. 'Peace', surely the most famous rose in the world, is renowned for its ready willingness to sport, which it did steadily after its introduction in 1945. It took 17 years for 'Chicago Peace' to come along, but the wait was worth it.

In the final words of my first book, *Growing Good Roses*, I admitted that the most beautiful rose I'd ever seen was an outlandishly long-stemmed, oversize blossom of 'Chicago Peace' that came from my garden in San Francisco. That bloom remains in my mind's eye as pure perfection, and although I've seen many gorgeous roses since, nothing has surpassed it.

In many ways, 'Chicago Peace' is quite similar to its mother—bushes are similarly sized and grow to nearly identical heights, and the foliage of both varieties is dark green, leathery, and glossy. The key difference is color. While 'Peace' is basically golden to pale yellow with petals edged in rose-pink, 'Chicago Peace' is primarily phlox pink with the base of each of its 43 petals colored canary yellow.

When the dynamic hybridizing duo Christensen and Carruth crossed 'Bridal Pink' with an unnamed sister sibling of 'Lagerfeld', they had their sights on a good greenhouse rose. Alas, indoors, the offspring was nothing special. Then someone had the bright idea to try plants outside. Bingo!

Growing more vigorously in the garden than it ever might in greenhouses, bushes of 'Crystalline' reach 5-foot heights. Foliage is distinctive not only because of its rich, deep green color but also because the edges of the leaves are as uniformly serrated as fine culinary knives.

The ultimate reward for growing 'Crystalline' is harbored in its lovely white blossoms, which are fully double (to 35 petals each) and exquisitely formed, making 'Crystalline' a firebreather at the exhibition table at rose shows.

I was once severely chastised for referring to 'Crystalline' as a Grandiflora rather than a Hybrid Tea. The reason for that is because I fell for 'Crystalline' before 1987, the year it was introduced to commerce as a Hybrid Tea (because there is no category for Grandiflora roses in the greenhouse trade, where 'Crystalline' was intended to thrive).

Since we know that 'Crystalline' *should* be classified as a Grandiflora, just remember that it prefers blossoming in sprays rather than one-to-a-stem, and disbud as you see fit.

D A I N T Y   B E S S

Believing that they didn't last well as cut flowers, when I began growing roses I banned single-petaled roses from my garden. When a friend persuaded me to give 'Dainty Bess' a try, I learned just how wrong I had been. Introduced in 1925, 'Dainty Bess' has remained the most popular single-petaled Hybrid Tea ever since.

Although each blossom has only five petals, they're broad, wavy at their edges, and deliciously fragrant. Depending on weather, particularly the intensity of sunlight, petals range from silvery pink to dusky pink and surround dense clusters of maroon stamens—not a big deal unless you know that more than 90 percent of rose stamens are some shade of yellow.

Not only are individual blossoms notable, so is the way they present themselves, most often in sprays of three to five blooms each. Plants are worthy of mention, too—tall, upright, and well cloaked in disease-resistant foliage.

'Dainty Bess' is a must-have variety for those fond of cutting roses in tight bud. Not only needn't you wait until the sepals are thoroughly unfurled, you can safely harvest when only a couple of sepals have begun to turn down. The remainder will conclude their show in a vase while blooms continue to expand.

ELINA

It annoys me that I have to call this lovely rose by the name under which it's sold in the United States. In 1983 I saw it growing in Europe under the name 'Peaudouce', which is French for "soft skin." I thought the name thoroughly fitting, but those in charge of commercial nomenclature declared otherwise and introduced it to America the following year as 'Elina'. In my growing fields, it's still labeled 'Peaudouce', but if you want to order it from an American nursery, ask for 'Elina'. Whatever you choose to call it, this isn't merely a fine rose, it's an exemplary cut flower.

I'm always surprised when I remember that blossoms of 'Elina' have only 35 petals each, because blooms mature to sizes usually reserved for roses more heavily petaled. Other pluses include a natural habit for producing only one bloom per stem (the way good Hybrid Teas should) on exceptionally long cutting stems.

When we grade roses for sale at Garden Valley Ranch, we code them the same way they're ranked in rose shows—blue is top of the line, then red, and finally yellow. Bloom size and stem length are the benchmarks for grading. 'Elina' doesn't seem to believe it's okay sometimes to be less than blue-dot quality.

Although I've never been able to grow the fine Floribunda 'Evening Star' as well as friends in warmer climates do, because it's such a superb cut flower I wouldn't dream of being without it.

Bill Warriner, Jackson & Perkins's ace hybridizer, chose 'White Masterpiece' and 'Saratoga' to mother and father 'Evening Star'. Like its mother, 'Evening Star' is fully double and heavily petaled (the reason I can't grow it to its ultimate potential—because it needs more summer heat than I can provide). Like its father, 'Evening Star' is an exemplary Floribunda, freely giving of lovely sprays of sweetly scented blossoms that are primarily soft white with a hint of yellow at each petal's base. The greatest plus is that 'Evening Star' is more floriferous than either of its parents.

Foliage is large, dark green, and leathery. Bushes are particularly well shaped for a modern rose; vigorous, too.

'Evening Star' displays a marked preference for blossoming in sprays. Occasionally, of course, solitary buds form. If you have your heart set on one bloom per stem, you can disbud for that look. Just make certain to remove the smaller side buds surrounding the centermost (terminal) bud early in their development. If you wait until they near maturity, you're bound to leave telltale scars.

Because it's such a superb cut flower, I grow more 'Fair Bianca' in my cutting fields than any other of David Austin's lovely English roses. Florists can't seem to get enough of it.

Perhaps it's the color—as white as any rose of any age. Or maybe the form—reminiscent of roses far older (often compared to the classic Damask 'Madame Hardy'). Could be the fragrance—sumptuous and deep (supposedly like myrrh). Then again, it might be because mature blooms reveal an irresistible green button-eyed center. No, I believe the secret of success is harbored in the blossoms—they just don't give up, lasting a seeming eternity after harvest.

Plants are agreeable, too. Although the bushes tend to hug the ground, if you're not piggy about stem length of harvested blossoms, well-rounded plants can reach 3-foot heights.

'Fair Bianca' can be cut in reasonably tight bud and still be expected to open in a vase, but blossoms are nothing special at this stage. It's wiser to wait until the petal-packed rosettes begin to strut their stuff by revealing their shallow-cupped form. Don't wait so long that the green button-eyed center becomes apparent. That magnificent stage should be enjoyed well after harvest.

F A M E !

In the introduction to this chapter, I admitted that I had already written about some of the very best cut-flower roses in *All-America Roses*, the first book in this series. Although I'd vowed not to repeat myself, I must make an exception with 'Fame!' because no other rose I know can match its lasting power.

Keith Zary, the current star hybridizer for Jackson & Perkins, assures me that the vase life 'Fame!' enjoys is no accident, that its parents were chosen carefully with that very quality in mind.

A little-known rose introduced in 1963 as 'Zorina' was never a commercial success. Although officially designated as a greenhouse variety, 'Zorina' didn't perform exceptionally well as a plant, but its blossoms seemed to last an eternity. Was a secret to bloom longevity lurking there?

Zary hoped it was, but he knew that a robust plant was needed to support such blossoms. Consequently, he chose 'Tournament of Roses' (one of the best-behaved, most disease-resistant roses ever) as a mate for 'Zorina'.

I'm not quite certain what claims to make regarding the vase life of 'Fame!' I've seen it last three times as long as most rose blossoms, but just to be on the safe side I'll say that its blooms last only twice as long as those of any other rose I know.

It was only fitting that after breeding more winning Floribunda roses than any hybridizer in history, Gene Boerner was finally to have a rose named after him. That he hybridized it himself was also proper; no one else might have done such a fine job. In any case, he picked a doozy that has held up well (it is currently rated 8.5 by the American Rose Society, placing it soundly among roses deemed "excellent").

'Gene Boerner', a 1969 All-America winner, is registered as a medium pink Floribunda. In actuality, it's a pink blend, with colors on each blossom ranging from pastel to true rose-pink. Fragrance is no more than mild, but that seems oddly appropriate for a rose colored so delicately.

Vigorous, well-behaved, upright bushes sport abundant glossy foliage. Even though stems are rather thin, they're strong and they carry blossoms well even when expected to support large sprays.

Speaking of sprays, that's how Mr. Boerner prefers to display his blossoms, so if you're after one bloom per stem, look elsewhere (among the Hybrid Teas, roses with natural proclivities for one-to-a-stem display).

On the other hand, if sprays of soft pink roses please you, look no further— 'Gene Boerner' is a beauty and a fine tribute to its talented creator.

Here's a rose whose success testifies to the fallibility of the present All-America Rose Selection process. It was passed over in 1983 when 'Sweet Surrender' and 'Sun Flare' won instead. I predicted at the time that these two selections would be vague memories in another decade—one of my more accurate forecasts. Today 'Gold Medal' is rated higher than either 1983 "winner" by the voting members of the American Rose Society, as well it should be.

'Gold Medal' is one of the best-behaved of all roses—it does as it's told. If you like sprays of blossoms, you can have them with long stems. If you disbud properly, they're showstoppers. If-one-to-a-stem blooms are your preference, you can have them, too.

Buds are golden yellow with tawny edges, a color combination that persists through maturity, lightening in shade as blossoms age. Moderate fragrance is obvious from start to finish.

Roses that are early bloomers are always favorites, but so are varieties that persist into winter. 'Gold Medal' is one of the last roses to give up the ghost. Where I garden, some years, I've cut long-stemmed blossoms on Christmas Day.

All things considered, 'Gold Medal' wins my vote for the best yellow rose ever.

GRUSS AN AACHEN

Hybridized in 1909 by Geduldig, a little known German breeder, 'Gruss an Aachen' stumps rose antiquarians because they don't know how to properly classify the lovely thing. Many people would happily lay claim to it. Even David Austin lists it among his English roses, a move I find vaguely presumptuous, although I see his point. 'Gruss an Aachen' does indeed closely resemble some of Austin's own splendid creations, because the greatest of all attributes inherent to 'Gruss an Aachen' is that it looks like an heirloom rose of considerable antiquity but blossoms like a modern fool. Still, I concur with the American Rose Society's decision to label the rose a Floribunda— big deal; it doesn't really matter one hoot what you call it, only that you plant it.

Mature plants reach only moderate heights (rarely above 3 feet) but produce exceptionally large blossoms (to 3 inches across), both one per stem and, more often, in well-balanced sprays. The tough foliage is dark green and plants are exceptionally hardy to winter.

Blooms are sights to behold. Buds and immature flowers are pearly pink. As blossoms mature, they turn creamy-white and take on an obvious silky sheen. Fragrance is downright decadent throughout.

ICEBERG

The German family of Kordes has graced rosedom with some everlasting beauties. Ironically, 'Iceberg', surely the finest of their efforts, was one of their first. Introduced in 1958, it went around as 'Schneewittchen'. Since Americans could never be expected to wrap their tongues around so complicated a name, it made its American debut as 'Iceberg'. It has remained in the Floribunda foreground ever since and for a wealth of reasons, not the least of which is the longevity of its cut flowers.

Blossoms of 'Iceberg' are icy white and almost always appear in clusters of as few as 3 to as many as 12 flowers per stem. Although buds are lovingly formed and high centered, they flatten as they open. Light but definite fragrance lasts throughout, and foliage is clean, small, mid-to light green, and glossy.

Be forewarned that 'Iceberg' is a late bloomer, but there's an advantage to such timing. Since you never want all your roses of one color to bloom at exactly the same time, always choose varieties within color groups that stagger their blossoms over summer. When making such long range plans for white roses, count on 'Iceberg' to be the last to bloom both in spring and fall.

Prune bushes however you like, they're perfectly obedient.

The Danish hybridizing family of Poulsen didn't give us a clue about the heritage of 'Ingrid Bergman', registering her birth as a result of cross-pollinating two unnamed seedlings. Although I'd really like to know more, I happily accept the gift. Like her namesake, 'Ingrid Bergman' is a ravishing beauty.

Ms. Bergman was introduced to European commerce in 1984, but it took another 10 years for the rose to go through the rigors of strict quarantine restrictions before it could be sufficiently propagated for sale in the United States. After seeing the rose at the national headquarters of the British Royal Rose Society, I jumped the gun and ordered Ingrid from Canada, where there are no quarantine restrictions for importing roses. Now, thankfully, the red beauty is readily available from a myriad of sources, including your local nursery.

The dark red blossoms have 35 petals each, and not a single one is wasted in the creation of high-centered blooms whose petals quill at their edges as they mature. Just before opening fully, the mass of petals forms a well-shaped dome culminating in a pinpoint center.

Granted, the fragrance is nothing special for a red rose, but it's definite and it persists throughout bloom life. Foliage is appropriately handsome—dark green, leathery, and glossy; disease-resistant, too.

In *Miniature Roses*, an earlier book in this series, I pointed out that Miniature roses are among the best of all cut flowers. In general, they outlast their full-size relatives for days. None outperforms 'Jean Kenneally'.

Named for a fine southern California rosarian and hybridized by Dee Bennett of Tiny Petals Roses, 'Jean Kenneally' was introduced in 1984. The result of a cross between the Hybrid Tea 'Futura' and the Miniature 'Party Girl', 'Jean Kenneally' bears resemblance to both parents. Like 'Party Girl', blossoms are decidedly miniature. Like 'Futura', bushes are tall and blossoms have Hybrid Tea form.

If you're in search of a Miniature rose to plant at the edge of a garden as a border, look elsewhere, because 'Jean Kenneally' often grows taller than 2 feet. On the other hand, if your quest is a Mini that lasts well as a cut-flower, look no further. Presently, 'Jean Kenneally' enjoys a 9.5 rating (10.0 is perfect) by voting members of the American Rose Society.

Registered as an apricot blend, 'Jean Kenneally' blossoms are indeed a wondrous combination of shades of apricot. Besides being well formed, blooms show a decided preference for presenting themselves in clusters, rather than one-to-a-stem. Not only are sprays frequent, they occur on long cutting stems.

I call 'Just Joey' the "something-for-everyone" rose because everybody loves it. Heirloom aficionados appreciate its mature form and grace, while modern enthusiasts cherish its everblooming habits. Everyone, of course, admires its powerful fragrance.

The American Rose Society calls 'Just Joey' an orange blend; I call it buff-apricot, heavy on the apricot. Whatever the classification, color is deepest when blooms are in bud. As they open their 30 petals, blossoms lighten in color and they grow in size well after harvest.

Plants of 'Just Joey' are nothing to brag about. After crops of blossoms are harvested, bushes look downright puny and sorely lacking in vigor. In truth, they're little bloom factories churning out flower after flower throughout summer.

Don't let the relatively spindly stems of 'Just Joey' make you doubt their ability to hold blossoms erect. Even when they're crooked, stems are strong enough to display their blooms well. Foliage is notable, too, and not just because it's large. Until just before blossoms mature, leaves are strongly tinted mahogany; as they age, they turn dark, shiny green.

Not only do flowers last well, if preservatives are added to the water in vases, blooms reach the size of dinner plates and never lose a whiff of fragrance.

Although David Austin's hybridizing palette is widely colored, the majority of his progeny are pastel. For a while, red in particular seemed to elude Mr. Austin; 'Othello' is just as purple as it is crimson, and, albeit beautifully colored, 'The Squire' has unsatisfactory growth habits.

Hoping to retain color and improve plant habit, Austin crossed the awkward Squire with 'Mary Rose', one of his best-behaved shrubs. This well-reasoned approach to creating new roses resulted in the exceptionally lovely 'L. D. Braithwaite', proving once and for all that red roses have not escaped Austin.

Braithwaite's color isn't merely pure crimson, it doesn't fade as petals age (or, worse yet, take on opaque shades of blue, the way many modern hybrids do). Bloom form is a bit loose, but many people find such casualness thoroughly appealing. No one quibbles with the fine fragrance that persists from buds to fully open flowers.

Like those of its mother 'Mary Rose', shrubs of 'L. D. Braithwaite' are almost model; they have a tendency to spread nearly as wide as they grow tall, but their overall look is shapely. Foliage is nothing special, but it's at least abundant and reasonably resistant to disease.

Even the most devoted of Austin's fans admit that they wish his roses bloomed more steadily. For an Austin, 'L. D. Braithwaite' is prolific.

Named for the teenage Nashville singing sensation, 'LeAnn Rimes' was introduced to commerce in 1998. I'd already grown it for two years, however, since it was an entry among the Hybrid Tea roses being considered for an All-America award in the year 2000. Although it didn't win, it scored well, and it was my personal pick for the coveted award.

It's yet unclear whether Miss Rimes will be color classified as a yellow-blend or a pink-blend; either is possible, since both colors are in strong evidence, varying in intensity at different times of the year and, of course, in varying climates. In Petaluma, California, 'LeAnn Rimes' is definitely a pink blend, although yellow is always present. So is powerful fragrance.

LeAnn is a tall lass; to 8 feet, I'm told. I'll never let my plants get that tall, keeping them in bounds with moderately severe pruning in winter and harvesting with abandon (the longer the stems the better) in summer.

Comments from other All-America judges around the country prove that 'LeAnn Rimes' is notably hardy. Foliage is good, too—abundant and reasonably resistant to disease.

As well-behaved Hybrid Teas should, 'LeAnn Rimes' almost always presents her blossoms one to a stem. Harvest them when sepals are down and outer petals have just begun to separate.

When 'Maggie Barry' was introduced in 1996, I chose not to plant it (even though I knew it had been hybridized by the enormously talented Sam McGredy of New Zealand) because it was being touted as orange, not one of my favorite colors.

Then a southern California rosebuddy whose opinion I respect told me I was missing out on a good bet for a fine cut-flower rose. "Besides," he claimed, "it's not orange, it's coral-pink. Think of it as a coral 'Color Magic'." Since 'Color Magic' is my favorite all-time rose, that was all I needed to hear.

Even though I love what I've seen, I don't believe 'Maggie Barry' will ever quite aspire to the glories of 'Color Magic'. First, it's not as wondrously colored (although it is flashy). Second, the fragrance isn't even close. True, it's distinctly scented, but not as seductively as 'Color Magic'.

On the other hand, in some ways it's even better than my favorite rose. Bushes are more vigorous (often to 5 feet) and blossoms occur steadily rather than in flushes. Also, because she seems to know that her blooms are prettiest one to a stem, 'Maggie Barry' rarely needs disbudding. Finally, 'Maggie Barry' is as floriferous as one could hope for in a modern Hybrid Tea.

All things considered, I think I'll keep her.

MAGIC CARROUSEL

Ralph Moore of Visalia, California, hybridized so many winning Minis that he's been nicknamed the "father of modern Miniature roses." Although he bred 'Magic Carrousel' more than a quarter century ago, it remains one of his triumphs.

As is so often the case with roses, the key to success is the color of the blossoms, in this case the combination of colors. Petals are basically yellowish white with edges tinged red. The degree of tinging varies by season, being deepest in fall. Even in the heat of summer, however, colors aren't bleached and blossoms are eye-catching. They're also high-centered and beautifully formed, with 35 petals per bloom. Though flowers occasionally appear one to a stem, they more frequently form in clusters. Either way, they're keepers.

Foliage is appropriately small and also leathery, glossy, and notably resistant to disease. Plants are vigorous and bushy.

That very vigor is what keeps 'Magic Carrousel' out of some gardens, because this variety shows no modesty where height is concerned, meaning that it won't do as a low-growing border the way many Minis will. Contented plants of 'Magic Carrousel' quickly grow taller than 2 feet—which is not a disadvantage, simply be forewarned.

As good Minis should, 'Magic Carrousel' makes an ideal container plant.

MINNIE PEARL

I was in the audience at the Grand Ole Opry in the summer of 1982 when Sarah Ophelia Colley Cannon (famously known as Minnie Pearl) was given a bouquet of the roses that bear her stage name. Harmon Saville, the hybridizer, made the presentation, and Minnie was beside herself. She'd be even more thrilled to know how well the rose has borne the test of time. Currently rated 9.5 by the voting members of the American Rose Society (10.0 is perfect), 'Minnie Pearl' is formidable both at the show table and in the garden.

Except for the size of her blossoms, not much is miniature about 'Minnie Pearl'. Plants are tall and vigorous—qualities expected in Miniature roses that serve double duty as good cut flowers. In that regard, 'Minnie Pearl' is a trooper.

Although the American Rose Society has registered 'Minnie Pearl' as a pink blend, she's much more. Pink is there, to be sure, but so are coral and apricot, the combination of which is winning from spring through fall.

Like the two other Miniature roses in this book that are famed for their qualities as cut-flowers ('Jean Kenneally' and 'Magic Carrousel'), 'Minnie Pearl' produces blossoms that are tenacious; they also occur more frequently in sprays than one-to-a-stem. Disbud as you like—they're plentiful.

N E W   D A Y

'New Day', a European transplant, was hybridized by the German team of Kordes and introduced to commerce in 1977 as 'Mabella', the name it's still known by in Europe. Those in charge of rose nomenclature decided on the new name when the rose made its American debut.

Although its blossoms are admired for their fragrance and larger-than-usual size, it's their mimosa-yellow coloring that has put 'New Day' on the map. Because clear yellow Hybrid Tea roses that last well as cut flowers are difficult to find, I predict 'New Day' will remain in the foreground until something better comes along to take its place. So far, I haven't spotted a contender.

Lest you believe 'New Day' is the perfect yellow rose, however, there are certain faults you should know about. As with many other yellow roses, vigor is disappointing, especially for a Kordes rose (they are more often too vigorous). Moreover, stem length is highly variable, ranging from shorter than you'd like to longer than is strictly necessary. Still, those qualities sit well with flower arrangers, who don't want all roses to grow on stems of identical lengths. Ultimately, however, the clear, nonfading color makes such shortcomings seems nearly irrelevant.

Gardeners who face strong summer heat should know that 'New Day' holds up well even where summers are scorchers.

P L A Y B O Y

I was never a fan of orange roses until I met 'Playboy' (which technically isn't orange, rather an orange blend). Bronze buds open quickly to form blossoms whose petals are randomly splashed orange, yellow, and scarlet. I know that may sound unappealing, but just wait until you see 'Playboy' strut his stuff. The fact that blooms are seductively fragrant doesn't hurt one bit, nor does their extended vase life.

Although blossoms may have as many as 10 petals (more frequently, 7), gardeners think of 'Playboy' as a single rose because it can't wait to show off its handsome boss of stamens. Because of the relatively light petalage and its rush to unfurl, stems of 'Playboy' can be cut when buds are tight. Don't worry if sepals aren't yet folded down (certainly not all of them); the floral show happily concludes in a vase. As good Floribundas should, 'Playboy' almost always presents its blossoms in sprays.

I know people who swear they'd grow 'Playboy' for its foliage alone, a claim I perfectly understand. Not only is it adamantly resistant to disease, it's so glossy green that it looks hand-polished.

If you can bear to leave the last roses of summer on bushes of 'Playboy', you'll be rewarded in fall with a smashing crop of hips.

PRECIOUS PLATINUM

I'm forever indebted to this variety because it's the reason I began to write about roses. In 1984 an esteemed rosarian from Ireland wrote an article lamenting the loss of fragrance in red roses. He listed 'Precious Platinum' among the scentless. One of us was wrong. I took another sniff and wrote an article called "Whose Nose Knows," and I haven't stopped writing since.

Fragrance aside, blossoms of 'Precious Platinum' are precious indeed; they not only last an eternity, they reach gigantic proportions before they call it a day. They also retain their cardinal-red color well throughout maturity.

Be forewarned, however, of the bushes on which 'Precious Platinum' flowers. They are exceptionally vigorous and reach greater heights than do most Hybrid Teas. On the other hand, they produce their flowers on amazingly long cutting stems and rarely need disbudding.

Because blooms are heavily petaled, give them extra time to mature before harvesting them. While most Hybrid Teas can be cut when their sepals are down and the first row of petals begin to separate themselves from others, for 'Precious Platinum', two rows should be obvious. Otherwise their showy display won't properly conclude.

Another notable attribute of this rose is petal substance—as thick and touchy-feely as that of any rose I know.

When Tosh Nakashima won an All-America award in 1988 for his Grandiflora 'Prima Donna', I feared that the rose wouldn't last in commerce. Fuchsia-pink roses already existed and the ones that stood the test of time were richly fragrant. Alas, the scent of 'Prima Donna' was only mild. It had a trick up its sleeve, however—an ability to last particularly well after harvest. Other pluses came with exhibition-quality blossoms that verged on being oversize.

Because blossoms are composed of only 27 petals each, they can safely be cut in tight bud. Sepals should be down, but rows of petals needn't separate themselves from others. In fact, blooms needn't even be "cracked" (a floral term to denote blossoms that have begun unfurling their petals).

The tall shrubs on which 'Prima Donna' flowers are exemplary. They're naturally urn-shaped and well clothed in large, midgreen, semiglossy foliage.

'Prima Donna' is a favorite among rosarians who like exceptionally long stems—longer than 2 feet more often than shorter. As long as you follow the cardinal rule of cutting above a five-leaflet set of foliage facing outward from the center of the bush, you should cut stems as long as possible. Otherwise plants will become gangly as they soar through summer.

P R I S T I N E

The late William Warriner of Jackson & Perkins was the most prodigious American hybridizer ever. Although his 'Color Magic' is my personal favorite, I predict that history will record 'Pristine' as Warriner's finest triumph. On the other hand, many people will question why 'Pristine' is listed here.

"It blows too fast," they complain, referring to the fact that blossoms of 'Pristine' open quickly after harvest. That's true, but the real problem is that people cut blossoms too late. With only 28 petals per blossom, flowers should be cut in tight bud with full expectations of blooms maturing fully in a vase.

The blossoms of 'Pristine' and the bush on which they flower are a true paradox. The vigorous plants have thick, tough thorns and exceptionally large foliage. Conversely, the blossoms are the essence of delicacy in both form and color. The sweetly scented, light pink, wavy petals have edges that seem to have been dipped in darker pink.

'Pristine' is classified as a Hybrid Tea, which it should be. Occasionally, however, stems appear with a cluster of buds on their tips. You can disbud for only one blossom, of course, but consider instead removing the terminal (largest and centermost) bud and see what happens when the others are left to develop—a showstopping bouquet.

PURPLE TIGER

The sassy Floribunda 'Purple Tiger' was introduced to rosedom at large in 1991, but I grew it two years before as a test plant. Although I suspected that florists wanted roses in new colors, I had no idea how desperate they were for a mixture of purple and mauve-pink striations with white flecks. Floral arrangers went nuts and I added large numbers of plants to my growing fields. I've never regretted it.

Besides its outlandish coloring, 'Purple Tiger' has other attributes key to its success. First, as a good Floribunda should, 'Purple Tiger' carries its blossoms in sprays. Second, foliage is glossy and stems are almost thornless. Finally, blooms have a wondrous casual appeal, in part because petalage is so widely varied (blooms may have anywhere from as few as 26 to as many as 40 petals each). Fragrance is all but absent, but hey, let's give it a break.

Plants grow relatively low and give the overall appearance of being incapable of much flower production. In fact, they're little bloom factories. Although stems are comparatively thin, they are strong and have no difficulty holding their clusters of blossoms erect.

Be gentle when you prune 'Purple Tiger' and never remove more than half its dormant wood; better yet, only slightly more than one-third.

ROYAL SUNSET

I'll never understand why 'Royal Sunset' isn't more highly praised, although it's obvious that someone besides myself appreciates it, because it enjoys a 9.2 rating by the American Rose Society. Still, it's in relatively restricted commerce and far too little known. In addition to being a gorgeous bloom that lasts well as a cut flower, it's a Climber! When you consider that it's also fragrant as all get-out, I'm utterly stumped over such a well-kept secret.

Assets are many. First, color. Blossoms are true apricot, not beigy or pinky. Second, fragrance, which is deeply ravishing. Third, shelf life. With only 20 petals per bloom, flowers can be cut in tight, tight bud. Not only will they surely open, they'll keep growing until they span up to 5 inches.

It seems obvious that hybridizer Dennison Morey had a climber in mind when he chose parents for 'Royal Sunset'; also that he hoped for yellow or some shade thereof, since he selected the yellow-blended, climbing 'Sutter's Gold' to father his child and the clear, bright yellow, climbing 'Sungold' as its mother. He not only got a plant that outclimbs either parent, he was rewarded with a color second to none.

Plants are obedient and foliage is sensational—dark green and as finely serrated as well-tooled leather.

Before writing another word, I'm compelled to admit that I'm thoroughly smitten by this rose. Keep that in mind as I try to temper my enthusiasm.

When British amateur hybridizer Robert Holmes hybridized 'Sally Holmes', he apparently hadn't a clue how wondrous an event had occurred. Not only did he not patent his find so that royalties from sales would be paid him, he didn't live to learn how overwhelmingly the rose world embraced his creation.

Although 'Sally Holmes' is registered as a Shrub rose, it grows as you train it. If you had a climber in mind, Sally obliges with spans of growth to 30 feet wide. If you yearn for a fountainous shrub (the way she actually prefers to grow), she responds well pruned to your favorite height.

Each fragrant blossom has only five petals, but they're broad and wide (up to 3 inches across) and always carried in sprays of large clusters on long, smooth stems. Buds are pale apricot, but as they age, petals gradually whiten—creamy at first, then pure white.

Cut sprays of 'Sally Holmes' even before you think you should (no more than one sepal need be unfurled). Vase life is astounding for a single-petaled rose.

SEA PEARL

I often complain about the names chosen for roses, usually that nothing about their growth habits or bloom characteristics has the slightest attribute in common with the name chosen for them. 'Sea Pearl' is an exception because it excels when cultivated near open waters.

Uncommonly tall for a Floribunda, bushes of Sea Pearl are lofty growers, reaching heights in excess of 5 feet in the course of each summer. In compensation for plants taller than you might like, stems are longer than you dreamed of and carry sprays of multiple blooms. Properly disbudded, 'Sea Pearl' is a feared competitor at rose exhibitions.

'Sea Pearl' is registered as a pink blend, but blossoms actually blend more peach than pink with shades of buff-yellow. Although fragrance isn't overpowering, it's definite and it persists throughout the life of each bloom.

It will do you no good to try to convince plants of 'Sea Pearl' to become less ambitious in their growth habits. If you prune them too low, they'll pout throughout the beginning of the next growth season, refusing to bloom before reaching the height at which they're comfortable.

Just plant it at the rear of a bed of roses and count on cutting stems that will tower over most others in a mixed bouquet.

S E X Y   R E X Y

I visited Sam McGredy in New Zealand in 1984, the same year he introduced 'Sexy Rexy', several years before the rose was made available in the United States. He told me that he'd like to hear my opinion of one of his new varieties, then led me to a growing field where 'Sexy Rexy' was in full bloom. As I recall, I literally gasped when I saw it, and so might you when you see well-grown plants of this sensational Floribunda.

Perhaps one of the finest attributes of 'Sexy Rexy' is that it has done wonders to unite two camps of rosarians—those devoted to heirloom roses and those fond of modern roses. Blossoms of 'Sexy Rexy' have the form and grace of old roses, but its plant is a blooming fool.

'Sexy Rexy' presents its floral display in huge clusters of blossoms on long cutting stems. Blooms are soft to medium pink and heavily petaled (usually 40 petals each). The individual sweetly scented flowers are rosette-shaped and take their own sweet time to open fully.

Bushes are exemplary—well-rounded yet shapely and smothered in shiny, dark green foliage that is adamantly resistant to disease.

As its name would imply, the rose is sexy indeed and has gone on to mother or father (roses are bisexual) hundreds of new hybrids.

Before you read another word about this rose, understand that it is not a modest plant. Hybridized by the German family of Kordes and proud of its heritage, shrubs of 'Sparrieshoop' grow to the size of Volkswagens. Whatever its size, 'Sparrieshoop' freely doles out some of the best cut-flower roses in the garden.

Although I respect its grandiose wishes to flourish, I've learned that such aspirations are obedient to training. So I grow my 'Sparrieshoop' as short climbers on trellis fences 5 feet tall. At pruning time, I cut canes back to the top of the trellis. Summer's growth exceeds such height limitations, of course, but never to the point that my shears can't reach the base of the long-stemmed sprays of bloom.

Each blossom of 'Sparrieshoop' is composed of only five petals, but they're exceptionally broad and wavy. When fully open, the sharply fragrant, clear pink flowers reach 4-inch spans and reveal stamen-packed hearts of pure gold.

Almost everyone who sees 'Sparrieshoop' in bloom for the first time asks the same thing: "Is that a rose? It looks like a huge apple blossom." It's a rose all right; what a rose!

Show off your harvesting acumen by cutting stems of blossoms just after buds show color, before sepals begin unfurling. Properly conditioned, they surely will.

The only exception we make to selling our rose blossoms solely to the wholesale floral trade is for brides who are getting married at the ranch. Since they all want to include roses in their bridal-party bouquets, we let them walk through the growing fields to make their selections. Almost all skid to a halt when they get to 'Summer Fashion', which seems to shout, "Choose caressable me, I'm the one you want to carry down the aisle."

No other rose blends pale yellow with pink quite like 'Summer Fashion'. When petals first unfurl, pink is confined to their edges. As blossoms mature, pink becomes dominant.

I believe the reasons that 'Summer Fashion' presently is rated only 7.6 by the American Rose Society (still placing it high among roses considered "good") are that its stems are on the short side of average and are heavily thorned. I consider neither complaint worthy of such a low rating; I'd give it a 9.0—it's my hands-down favorite Floribunda.

If you're determined to have one bloom per stem, you can, of course, disbud for that look. I would encourage you, however, to allow 'Summer Fashion' to blossom as it prefers—in heart-stopping sprays of three to seven blooms each.

S U M M E R ' S   K I S S

In 1992, the French hybridizing firm House of Meilland introduced a rose named 'Paul Ricard', honoring the creator of an anise-based aperitif, which when mixed with water and ice is known as pastis. Thought to harbor a scent comparable to that of the liqueur, the rose enjoyed immediate success in Europe, winning awards in Rome, Saverne, and Lyon.

Because the Ricard name is known in America primarily only by chic cocktail groups, when the rose was introduced in the United States, the name was changed to 'Summer's Kiss'. It enjoyed only a limited release in 1996 but is now widely available.

The main reason 'Summer's Kiss' is a sure-bet winner is the color of its flowers. Buds are rich amber; as petals unfurl, they turn soft butterscotch. Fragrance is outrageous, supposedly of anise (my nose hasn't managed to substantiate that claim, but it likes what it smells).

When I read that blossoms of 'Summer's Kiss' are composed of 40 to 45 petals each, I worried that blooms wouldn't open well in my relatively cool summer climate. I shouldn't have. Perhaps because this variety was bred in the paradisiacal Mediterranean climate of Cap d'Antibes, blooms mature beautifully even where summers are chilly.

Stems are long, foliage is dense, and flowering is abundant.

S U N S E T   C E L E B R A T I O N

Although Gareth Fryer had already hybridized several fine roses, notably the handsome 'Bobby Charlton', he won his first All-America Rose award in 1998 with his lovely 'Sunset Celebration'.

Named in honor of the 100th anniversary of the enormously popular *Sunset* magazine, 'Sunset Celebration' has a bright future. As with the last-mentioned rose, 'Summer's Kiss', the key to success is color; in this case a miraculous blend of soft apricot and peachy pink.

Another variety that opens well even in mild climates, 'Sunset Celebration' is fully petaled (sometimes producing more than 35 petals per blossom). Still, blooms can be cut in relatively tight bud. Sepals should be fully reflexed, but petals needn't be clearly separated in rows from each other (at least no more than the first row).

Boasting model Hybrid Tea habits, blooms almost always occur one to a stem and rarely need disbudding. Foliage is deep green and well spaced. Stems are moderately long and flowers enjoy an extended vase life.

Watch for blossoms of 'Sunset Celebration' on awards tables at rose competitions. It's inevitable; blooms are high centered and have classic exhibition form, including petals that quill at their edges as blossoms mature. Although fragrance is only mild, it's pleasantly fruity.

All in all, this rose is a fine cause for celebration.

S W A N

David Austin has hybridized scads of white roses, but where good cut-flower roses are concerned, 'Swan' is my pick of the litter. About three-quarters on their way to full maturity, blossoms go into a holding pattern, then last and last before fully maturing, handily outliving other white roses in a mixed bouquet.

Although the mother of 'Swan' was an unnamed seedling, the father was the world-class 'Iceberg'. So a good bush is no surprise. It's quite tall, however, but it responds well to harvests of exceptionally long-stemmed blossoms.

Flower form is unique. Blooms aren't exactly shaped like rosettes but neither are they perfectly quartered; rather, an appealing combination of both. Flowers are uncommonly large and basically pure white with buff shadings.

Honesty compels me to alert those of you who live in damp climates that 'Swan' doesn't take well to rain. When rainfall is abundant, blossoms "ball" (a floral term meaning that blooms refuse to unfurl their petals). Even if rain is only slight, however, petals spot. So if rain is in the forecast, harvest blooms sooner than you otherwise might. Properly conditioned, they'll probably mature in a vase. Left on the bush, they're bound to freckle.

Other rosarians rave about the fragrance of 'Swan'. I find 'Swan' only moderately perfumed, but I marvel at its buxom blossoms.

For some bizarre reason, many gardeners don't believe that heirloom roses make good cut flowers. That's utter nonsense, of course. In the companion book to this one in the *A Passion for Roses* series, *Heirloom Roses*, I talk about more than 100 varieties of heirloom roses that make fine cut flowers. None, however, outperform the Bourbons and for more than one reason. Besides lasting gloriously when fresh, whole blossoms dry exceptionally well and hold their color, making them favorites for people fond of brewing potpourri.

'Variegata di Bologna' is a fine member of the family, but like her siblings, she knows no modesty in growth habits. Cultivated as a conventional shrub, plants quickly scramble 5 to 6 feet. Afforded support, when grown as climbers, plants reach 10-foot heights. If they're properly propped against a fence, growth may well span beyond 20 feet.

'Variegata di Bologna' isn't subtly striped. The base color of each blossom is creamy white, but petals are madly striped with crimson and purple. If a more modest striped Bourbon appeals to you, have a look at 'Honorine de Brabant', which is softly shaded lilac and mauve.

Because blossoms are heavily petaled, don't harvest them too soon. There's plenty of life left after the first three rows of intensely fragrant petals have separated from each other.

WHITE DELIGHT

I know perfectly well that I should never allow the name of a rose to influence my willingness to give it a try, but somehow or other in 1989 when 'White Delight' was introduced, the name turned me off. What's worse, I did this knowing that it had been bred by Bill Warriner, my all-time favorite (so far) hybridizer. Once I'd gotten a load of 'White Delight' for myself, however, I swore never again to allow the name of a rose to sway me.

Although 'White Delight' is unarguably delightful, white often has little to do with it. In fact, blossoms are actually white only when summer days are on the hot side of warm. Otherwise, when buds form, their outside petals are pinky green. As blossoms mature, the insides of the petals are porcelain pink.

Bushes are tough; canes are heavy and sport large, handsome thorns. Quintessentially Hybrid Tea, blossoms almost always appear singly and on admirably long cutting stems. Fragrance is perfectly acceptable.

A final plus that elevates 'White Delight' above other good white cut-flower roses is its stubborn floriferousness. Not only are blossoms abundant, they repeat themselves enthusiastically.

In my climate, bushes reach 5-foot heights. My rosebuddy Dan Bifano tells me that in Santa Barbara his reach 8 feet, but I believe he's exaggerating by at least a foot.

I N D E X